MARY
Queen of Scots

Sheila Watson

Wayland

Titles in the series

Elizabeth I
Henry VIII
James VI/I
Mary Queen of Scots
Queen Victoria
William I

Series editor: Sarah Doughty
Book editor: Katie Orchard
Consultant: Kayte Wallace
Designer: Jean Wheeler
Production controller: Carol Stevens

First published in 1995 by Wayland (Publishers) Ltd
61 Western Road, Hove, East Sussex, BN3 1JD, England

British Library Cataloguing in Publication Data
Watson, Sheila
Mary Queen of Scots. – (Kings and Queens series)
I. Title II. Series
941.105092

ISBN 0 7502 1447 3

Typeset by Jean Wheeler
Printed and bound in Milan, Italy by Rotolito Lombarda S.p.A.

Cover: A sixteenth-century portrait of Mary Stuart. Artist unknown.

Picture acknowledgements:
By kind permission of His Grace the Duke of Atholl 4 (bottom); Bridgeman Art Library (Giraudon) *cover*, 5 (photograph: John Bethell), 8 (British Museum), 10 (Musée Conde) top, 15 (Private Collection) bottom; English Heritage 19 (top); ET Archive (Bibliothèque Nationale de France) 6, 16 (bottom); Mary Evans 7 (bottom); Hamilton Collection at Lennoxlove 18, 26 (top); Robert Harding 20, 21 (bottom); Andrew Hayden *back cover*; Historic Scotland 17; Jersey Museums Service 24; National Library of Scotland 7 (top); National Portrait Gallery 9 (bottom), 10 (bottom), 22 (top), 28 (both); National Trust 19 (bottom), 21 top; National Trust for Scotland 22; By kind permission of His Grace the Duke of Norfolk 27; Ann Ronan 25; The Royal Collection © Her Majesty The Queen 12 (both); Scottish National Portrait Gallery 14, 16 (top), 22 (bottom), 26 (bottom); Scottish Record Office 15 (top); By Courtesy of the Dean and Chapter of Westminster Abbey 29 (bottom); David Williams Picture Library 13. All remaining pictures are from the Wayland Picture Library.
Artwork by Peter Bull 29 (top).

Contents

The Early Years

(Above) Mary as a prisoner of Queen Elizabeth. This picture was painted after Mary's death.

Mary's mother and father, Mary of Guise and James V.

Mary Stuart, Queen of Scots, was told on 7 February 1587 that she would be executed early the next day. She had been found guilty of plotting the death of Queen Elizabeth I of England, whose prisoner she had been for nearly nineteen years. The following morning she went bravely and calmly to her death, saying to her servants, 'You ought to rejoice and not to weep for that the end of Mary Stuart's troubles is now done.' How had Mary, once Queen of both Scotland and France, come to such a tragic end?

Linlithgow Palace, West Lothian, Scotland, where Mary was born.

When Mary was born in December 1542, her father, King James V of Scotland was dying, a broken man. He had been defeated the month before, by the English, at the battle of Solway Moss. On hearing of the birth of his daughter Mary – his heir – James said that she would lose the Scottish throne. He died soon afterwards and Mary became Queen of Scotland at only six days old.

The greatest threat came from Henry VIII, who wished Mary to marry his son Edward. Through this marriage, he would be able to bring Scotland under English rule. He tried to make the Scots agree to this by force and, even after he died in 1547, English attacks upon Scotland continued. In 1548, Mary was sent to France, her mother's homeland, for safety.

IMPORTANT DATES

1542   Mary is born. James V dies and his daughter Mary becomes Queen of Scotland.

1543   Treaties of Greenwich: Henry VIII arranges for Mary to marry his son, Prince Edward of England. Scottish Parliament rejects the Treaties of Greenwich.

1547   Henry VIII of England dies, and his son becomes King Edward VI of England.

1548   Mary sails for France.

A portrait of Mary and her first husband Francis II.

IMPORTANT DATES

1558 *Mary and the Dauphin Francis marry. Elizabeth I becomes Queen of England.*

1559 *Francis II becomes King of France with Mary as his Queen.*

1560 *Mary's mother dies. Francis II dies.*

1561 *Mary leaves France and returns to Scotland.*

Mary was only five years old when she went to live in France. Her mother, Mary of Guise, stayed behind to rule Scotland. Mary must have found France very strange for she spoke no French at first. However, she was made welcome at the French court and was brought up with the children of King Henri II of France in very grand surroundings. She shared a bedroom with the French princess Elisabeth, who became like a sister to her.

Mary was betrothed to Henri II's oldest son, the **Dauphin** Francis, in 1548. He was a year younger than Mary. Unlike Mary, Francis was a sickly child. Fortunately, Mary loved him and they were married when Francis was fourteen years old and Mary was fifteen. A few months later, Elizabeth Tudor, a **Protestant**, became Queen of England. Henri II immediately claimed that Elizabeth was not the rightful ruler of England. Instead, he put forward the claim of Mary, who was related to the English royal family and also a **Roman Catholic**. Elizabeth was furious and always saw Mary as a dangerous rival.

In 1559, Francis became King of France with Mary as his Queen. Only a year later, Mary's mother and husband both died, so she no longer ruled France. She had also lost the two people she loved most. There was no longer a place for her in France. She had to return to Scotland, a place that she hardly knew.

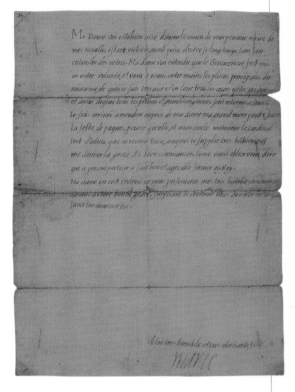

A letter written by Mary to her mother. She writes in French and signs herself Marie.

Henri II lies dying. Mary is standing at the foot of his bed and looking at him. Notice the doctors mixing medicines on the table.

Mary in Scotland

Mary found Scotland strange. It was very different from the France she knew and loved. Scotland was a poor country with few large towns. There were great differences between the lives of people in different areas of Scotland. However, she was determined to rule it well. Many Scots were Protestants and she was a Roman Catholic. Other rulers sometimes put to death **subjects** who would not follow their religion, but Mary **tolerated** the Protestants. She even allowed one of their leaders, John Knox, to argue the Protestant case before her, though she was afraid of his influence over the Protestants. He believed that people should put their obedience to God before their loyalty to a queen.

IMPORTANT DATES

1561 Mary announces that she will allow Protestants to continue to worship as they like, although she remains a Roman Catholic.

1565 Mary marries Henry, Lord Darnley.

1566 Riccio is murdered.

1566 Mary leads her troops into Edinburgh.

John Knox disliked women rulers and was not afraid to argue face to face with Mary.

Mary wearing white. White was the colour of mourning in France.

Mary was young, lively and charming. She enjoyed hunting and archery, and was a very good dancer. Soon the Scots cheered their beautiful, young queen wherever she went. Mary needed to marry again so she could have a child and heir to her throne. She had many **suitors**, most of whom were unsuitable. Elizabeth I of England was afraid that Mary would marry a foreign prince and become too powerful. She suggested Mary should marry her favourite, Robert Dudley, Earl of Leicester. He was handsome, intelligent and brave, but Mary rejected him. Unfortunately, her own choice was disastrous.

Robert Dudley, Earl of Leicester. Mary rejected him as a husband.

Mary's second husband, Henry, Lord Darnley, made her very unhappy.

Mary chose Henry, Lord Darnley to be her second husband. She was charmed by his good looks and called him 'the best-proportioned long man' she had ever seen. Unfortunately, she did not realize how selfish and thoughtless he was until it was too late.

Few people approved of her choice. Elizabeth I saw this marriage as Mary's attempt to strengthen her claim to the English throne, because Darnley had English royal blood in his veins. She was furious. Many Scottish nobles also resented Darnley's new importance.

Elizabeth I of England at her coronation. She always feared that Mary would take her crown.

Mary was very much in love when she married Darnley in 1565. However, she soon lost all respect for him. He was not older than nineteen when he married the twenty-two-year-old Mary. He was rude, proud and lazy. Mary gave him the title of King but kept all the real power to herself, and he resented this. Soon, however, she was pregnant and looking forward to the birth of an heir to the throne. Mary had become very fond of her secretary, David Riccio, and she trusted him. Darnley was jealous, and some Scottish lords who disapproved of Mary's closeness to Riccio saw this as their opportunity to take control of Mary and gain power for themselves. She was unaware that she was in danger.

This family tree, showing the kings and queens of England and Scotland, shows how strong Mary's claim to the English throne really was.

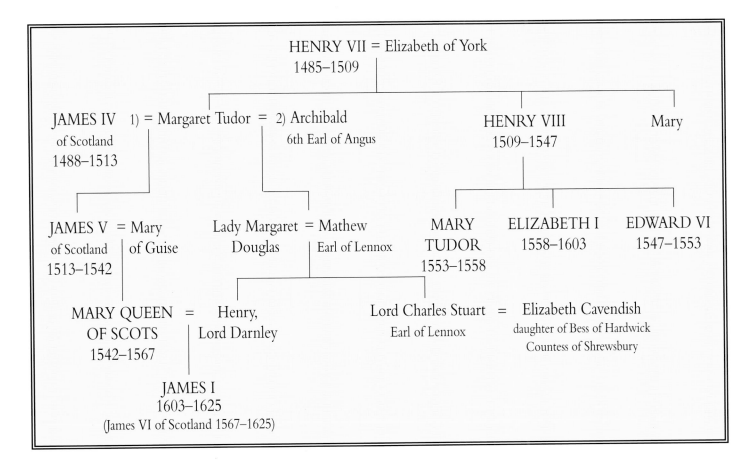

HENRY VII = Elizabeth of York
1485–1509

JAMES IV   1) = Margaret Tudor = 2) Archibald
of Scotland   6th Earl of Angus
1488–1513

HENRY VIII
1509–1547

Mary

JAMES V = Mary
of Scotland | of Guise
1513–1542

Lady Margaret = Mathew
Douglas | Earl of Lennox

MARY
TUDOR
1553–1558

ELIZABETH I
1558–1603

EDWARD VI
1547–1553

MARY QUEEN = Henry,
OF SCOTS | Lord Darnley
1542–1567

Lord Charles Stuart = Elizabeth Cavendish
Earl of Lennox   daughter of Bess of Hardwick
                    Countess of Shrewsbury

JAMES I
1603–1625
(James VI of Scotland 1567–1625)

One evening, when Mary was six months pregnant, she held a quiet supper party for her friends in her private rooms in Holyrood Palace. Darnley joined them unexpectedly, and then Lord Ruthven, a noble who was well known for his evil deeds, appeared at the door demanding Riccio. Suddenly, armed lords burst into the room. Darnley held Mary back while Riccio begged her to save him. Riccio was dragged out, murdered and thrown down the stairs.

(Above) The supper room, from which Riccio was dragged to his death.

Private stairs which linked Darnley's rooms to Mary's. Darnley and Ruthven used these stairs to join the supper party.

Over fifty stab wounds were found on his body. The terrified Queen was locked away in her room for two days.

Mary always believed the **conspirators**, including her husband, hoped she would be so frightened by Riccio's murder that she would have the baby too early and die herself. The lords would then rule through Darnley.

Certainly, if she lived, they planned to imprison her until her child was born and then rule on its behalf. But they **underestimated** her courage and determination. Darnley was soon sorry for his part in the plot, as he believed he would be the next victim. Mary used him to help her escape.

Escaping at night, Mary and Darnley rode for five hours at great speed to reach the safety of Dunbar Castle, a terrible **ordeal** for a pregnant woman. Mary raised an army and led the troops herself into Edinburgh, defeating the traitors. Some of them fled to England, where they sought protection from Queen Elizabeth.

The ruins of Dunbar Castle, as it is today. Mary and Darnley fled here after Riccio's murder.

Mary's Downfall

King James VI as a boy. He became King of Scotland at the age of thirteen months. Mary last saw him when he was only ten months old.

When Mary's son James was born in June 1566, Elizabeth I was jealous. She was unmarried and had no children. 'The Queen of Scots is lighter of a fair son,' she commented, 'while I am but a **barren stock**.' Mary, however, still had many problems. Her health was poor and Darnley was threatening to leave Scotland to live in France. Then Darnley had **smallpox** and had to wear a mask to hide the **disfigurement** to his face. Despite their previous quarrels, Mary showed

IMPORTANT DATES

1566 Birth of James VI in Edinburgh Castle.

1567 Darnley is murdered.
Bothwell is found not guilty of Darnley's murder.
Mary marries Bothwell.
Mary surrenders to her enemies at Carberry Hill.
Mary is imprisoned at Loch Leven Castle.
Mary is forced to abdicate in favour of her son.
Mary's son is crowned King James VI of Scotland.

1568 Mary escapes from Loch Leven.
Mary flees to England.
Conference meets to consider Mary's part in Darnley's murder.

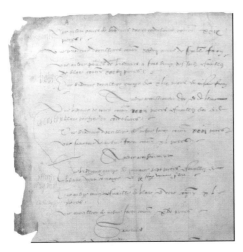

(Above) Part of Mary's will made just before James's birth. Childbirth was very dangerous then and she thought she might die.

him great kindness. She visited him several times in the house he was staying in at Kirk o'Field, in Edinburgh.

One night, after she had left him, the house was blown up. However, Darnley and his servant were found dead in the garden with no sign on their bodies of what had killed them. They were probably strangled, or suffocated trying to escape. Witnesses said they heard Darnley pleading for mercy. We still do not know who killed Darnley, though at the time some people believed that Mary was involved. Mary always said she was innocent of his murder. Others believed that the Earl of Bothwell and other conspirators had planned to blow up the house with Darnley in it and that Darnley had escaped, only to be murdered by Bothwell's helpers. Certainly, most people at the time believed Bothwell to have been the murderer.

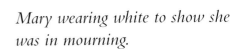

Mary wearing white to show she was in mourning.

Mary's third husband, James, Earl of Bothwell.

Bothwell was tried for the crime and found not guilty, though many still believed he was the murderer. However, he was determined to be King in Darnley's place. He persuaded some Scottish lords to support him, and forced Mary to go with him to Dunbar Castle. In May 1567, Bothwell divorced his wife and, just three months after Darnley's death, Mary and Bothwell were married in a Protestant service at Holyrood.

The marriage brought Mary little happiness. She had shocked her subjects and other monarchs because they believed that she had married her second husband's murderer. Nobody knows why she did it.

Mary surrenders herself to her enemies at Carberry Hill. This engraving was taken from a painting done in 1738.

She might have been forced by violence or she might have believed that Bothwell was strong and would help her keep the other lords under control.

She certainly did not expect people to react the way they did. The other lords were jealous of Bothwell's new power and rebelled, forming an army. At Carberry Hill (see page 16), Mary surrendered herself to them without a fight, on condition that Bothwell was allowed to go safely. She was imprisoned at Loch Leven Castle. Mary was pregnant with twins. With all the strain, she had a **miscarriage**. Weak and ill, she was forced to **abdicate**. Her thirteen-month-old son was crowned James VI of Scotland on 29 July 1567. Mary's enemies ruled on his behalf.

Loch Leven Castle. Mary's enemies accused her of being involved with the murder of Darnley to keep her imprisoned here after she abdicated.

Mary could expect no help from Bothwell. He fled abroad and died, mad, in prison in 1578. However, Mary escaped with the help of some of her supporters and managed to raise an army, but it was defeated by her Scottish enemies. In desperation, she fled to England and appealed to Elizabeth I for help.

Elizabeth felt she should help a fellow monarch, but was afraid that if she did, Mary would then harm her. Some Roman Catholics did not accept the Protestant marriage of Elizabeth's parents Henry VIII and Anne Boleyn. They believed that Mary, a Roman Catholic related to the English royal family, should be Queen of England. As Elizabeth did not have a child of her own to take over the throne, she worried that Mary's supporters might try to kill her and put Mary on the English throne.

The casket in which the Casket Letters were found. The original letters no longer exist.

Carlisle Castle, where Mary was kept for two months when she first came to England. It has changed a great deal since Mary's time.

Elizabeth refused to meet Mary and, set up an inquiry into the matter in 1568. The Scottish **Regent**, the Earl of Moray (Mary's half-brother), produced some letters that he claimed had been written by Mary. They were called the Casket Letters, and Mary's enemies claimed that they proved she and Bothwell had plotted together to kill Darnley. Mary was not allowed to give evidence in person and she could not prove that her subjects had rebelled unlawfully against her. Nothing was proved against her. It is now thought that the letters were forged.

While a prisoner, Mary's rooms were still well furnished. This French court cupboard is like one she might have had.

Imprisonment

I n 1569, Scotland was governed by the Scottish lords on behalf of the infant king, James. Elizabeth dared not let Mary go. She kept her a prisoner for nearly nineteen years. Elizabeth treated Mary well, but always had her guarded carefully.

For almost sixteen years George, Earl of Shrewsbury was Mary's gaoler. He moved her between places such as Tutbury Castle and Chatsworth House, to try to improve her health, but also to prevent her from escaping. Mary had over forty servants, who all had to be housed and fed. Among them were her own **physician**, several cooks and maids, a secretary and a master of the household. Although Elizabeth gave

IMPORTANT DATES

1569	*Northern Rebellion: Catholic rebellion in northern England to free Mary.*
1570	*Pope Pius V excommunicates Elizabeth I.*
1572	*Duke of Norfolk is executed for his part in the Ridolfi Plot.*
1583	*Throckmorton Plot.*
1585	*Mary has a new gaoler, Amyas Paulet.*
1586	*Babington Plot. Mary is arrested.*

Chatsworth House, where Mary was a prisoner, has been rebuilt since Mary's time.

Shrewsbury £52 a week (which was a very large sum of money at the time), he still had to pay many of their expenses himself.

Mary loved embroidery. She and Bess of Hardwick worked on these needlework pictures together.

(Below) Bess of Hardwick, wife of one of Mary's gaolers, who kept Mary company.

Mary's life was pleasant at times. Shrewsbury's wife, Bess of Hardwick, shared a love of embroidery and they often worked together on the same piece. She read and had visitors, played cards, and kept pets, such as small dogs and birds. Unfortunately her health was often poor. Sometimes she could barely walk and she was often in pain. She missed her son James very much. Above all, Mary wanted to be free to return to Scotland.

COUNTESS OF SHROESBURY

Mary Queen of Scots, painted after her death.

Thomas Howard, Duke of Norfolk was executed in 1572 for his attempts to free Mary and marry her.

Mary's friends soon began to plot to set her free and restore her to the Scottish throne. In February 1570 the Pope **excommunicated** Elizabeth, releasing all English Roman Catholics from their loyalty to her. Some Roman Catholics decided to try to overthrow Elizabeth and make Mary Queen of England. However, Elizabeth had an excellent spy network and always found out about the plans in time.

The Duke of Norfolk became involved in schemes to release Mary and marry her. In 1571 the Ridolfi Plot, named after its Italian organizer, cost Norfolk his life

Elizabeth I, Queen of England, painted during her lifetime. She has far more jewels and much richer clothing than Mary in the picture on the opposite page.

because he aimed to put Mary on the English throne in Elizabeth's place. He was executed in 1572 but Elizabeth refused to order Mary's death without definite proof that Mary supported these plots. She was **reluctant** to kill another queen. She also feared it would make her very unpopular with other European monarchs.

Encouraged by foreign Catholic support, Mary plotted secretly against Elizabeth. In 1583 Francis Throckmorton (an English Roman Catholic), was **tortured** to reveal details of a plan to put Mary on the English throne with the help of Spanish troops. Elizabeth's councillors and many English people so feared for the queen's safety that they signed a **bond** promising to bring about the death of anyone who tried to murder Elizabeth or gained from it.

Amyas Paulet, Mary's last gaoler. Elizabeth hoped he would arrange Mary's secret murder so she would not have to order a public execution for Mary. Paulet refused.

In April 1585 Mary had a new gaoler, Sir Amyas Paulet, who was much stricter than Shrewsbury had been. To Mary's dismay, he stopped her servants smuggling letters in and out for her. She was only allowed to communicate with the French **ambassador**, and Paulet read these letters. Mary did not realize that Elizabeth's **ministers** were trying to find proof that she was involved personally in plans to overthrow Elizabeth.

In December 1585 Mary was moved to Chartley Hall. She was told that her friends had found a way to smuggle letters in and out of the house in a beer barrel. It was a trap. Every letter was copied for Francis Walsingham, one of Elizabeth's ministers. A young English Catholic, Sir Anthony Babington, thought this was a safe way of sending messages. He wanted to murder Elizabeth and, with Spanish help, restore the Roman Catholic religion in England by force so Mary could be Queen. She agreed in a letter.

Walsingham was delighted. This was the proof he needed to have Mary found guilty of **treason**. Mary was arrested, and Babington and the other plotters confessed and were publicly executed. The problem now remained: what was Elizabeth to do with Mary? Mary protested that only a subject could be tried for a crime against his or her monarch, and that she was the subject of no one. However, she later agreed to a trial, in order to put her case publicly.

Violent public deaths were a common sight across Europe. Here, Protestants are being killed in the Netherlands.

Mary's End

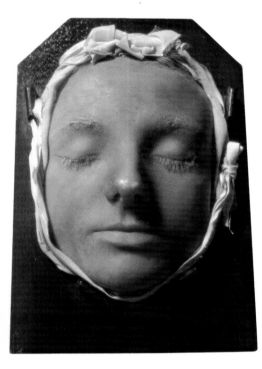

I n September 1586, Mary arrived at Fotheringhay Castle in Northamptonshire to await her trial. She had no lawyers to defend her and she was so ill she could hardly walk. She denied plotting to kill Elizabeth but said she had only tried to regain her own freedom. No one believed her and she was found guilty. The punishment was death, but Elizabeth was reluctant to sign the **death warrant** because she was worried about what other countries would think if she ordered Mary's execution. In February 1587 she finally signed it, after a great deal of pressure from her **councillors**.

(Above) Mary's death mask, showing what she looked like after her execution.

(Right) The axeman is just about to cut off Mary's head. Notice her belongings being burnt on the left of the picture.

Mary had several rosaries. This is one she gave to a friend just before she died.

Mary went bravely to her death on the morning of 8 February 1587. She pardoned her executioner and was helped to undress down to a red petticoat. Blindfolded, she knelt down to place her head on the block and said a prayer. The first blow of the axe did not kill her, but cut into her head. She was heard to murmur 'Sweet Jesus' and it took two more blows before her head was cut off. As the executioner held it up it fell from his hand, leaving him holding a wig. Mary's real hair was thin and grey. Her dog, who had hidden under her skirts, crawled out from under her body. It was covered in Mary's blood. Later, it refused to eat, and pined away.

IMPORTANT DATES

1586 *Mary is taken to Fotheringhay Castle to await trial.*

Mary is found guilty of plotting Elizabeth's death.

1587 *Mary is executed at Fotheringhay.*

1588 *Spanish Armada is defeated.*

1603 *Death of Elizabeth I. James VI, Mary's son, becomes King James I of England.*

Mary's clothes, the execution block and a **rosary** were all burnt to stop her supporters from keeping anything with her blood on it as a **relic**. Her body was wrapped in a lead coffin and later it was buried in Peterborough Cathedral.

Elizabeth was furious when she heard of the execution, because she had not wanted such a public death for Mary. She wore mourning clothes, although she was probably secretly relieved. However, she feared that Mary's son, or other European monarchs, might try to take revenge on her for Mary's death.

A portrait of Elizabeth I, painted to celebrate the defeat of the Armada.

James wanted to inherit the throne of England after Elizabeth, so he was prepared to forgive her. People in France and Spain were horrified at the news, but Londoners lit bonfires in the streets to celebrate. Philip II of Spain had already decided to attack England, and Mary's death made him even more determined to overthrow his enemy, Elizabeth. In 1588 he sent his great fleet of ships, the Armada, into battle against England, but it was defeated and wrecked.

Mary's son, James VI of Scotland, shown several years after he became James I of England.

A map showing some of the places connected with Mary Queen of Scots.

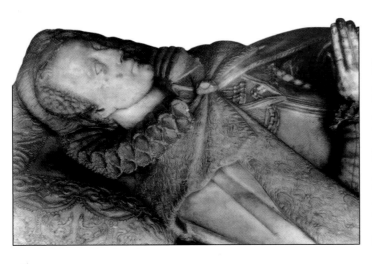

(Below) James had this monument placed over Mary's tomb in Westminster Abbey.

Elizabeth died of old age in 1603. She had no children, so Mary's son became King James I of England. He had his mother's body reburied in Westminster Cathedral along with many other kings and queens. In death, Mary Queen of Scots found the peace she had not found in life.

Glossary

abdicate To give up a throne so that someone else can be king or queen.

ambassador Someone who represents his or her country abroad.

barren stock Not able to have children.

bond A written agreement.

conspirators Plotters.

councillors A group of people who advise a monarch on how to run the country.

Dauphin The eldest son of the King of France, and heir to the French throne.

death warrant An official order to have someone killed.

disfigurement In smallpox, a scarring of the skin.

excommunicated Forbidden to have anything to do with the Roman Catholic Church. Roman Catholics are supposed to avoid anyone who has been excommunicated.

ministers Important officials who help to run the government.

miscarriage Having a baby too early so the baby is dead at birth.

ordeal A time when someone has to put up with great pain or trouble.

physician A doctor.

Protestant A Christian who does not believe that the Pope is head of the Church.

Regent Someone who rules and makes decisions on behalf of the king or queen because they are not old enough or able to do so themselves.

relic A holy souvenir.

reluctant Not willing to do something.

Roman Catholic A Christian who believes the Pope is head of the Church.

rosary A set of special beads sometimes used by Roman Catholics to help them count their prayers.

smallpox An illness which causes scars on the body. It can kill people who catch it.

subjects People who are ruled by a king, a queen or a government.

suitors People trying to convince someone else to marry them.

tolerated Put up with something.

tortured Forced to suffer great pain.

treason Plotting to harm the king or queen.

underestimated Not given enough credit for someone's qualities.

Further Information

Books to Read

Investigating the Tudors by A. Honey (The National Trust, 1993)
Mary, Queen of Scots by E. Melvin (Whigmaleerie, 1987)
Mary, Queen of Scots by S. Stepanek (Chelsea House, 1987)
Mary, Queen of Scots by D. Turner (Wayland, 1988, reprinted 1994)
Queen Elizabeth I by D. Turner (Wayland, 1987, reprinted 1994)
Queen of Scots by F. Macdonald (Macmillan/Piccolo, 1994)

Places to Visit

Carlisle Castle, Carlisle.
Mary was held prisoner here.

Chatsworth House, Derbyshire.
Completely rebuilt since Mary was a prisoner here.

Edinburgh Castle, Lothian.
Birthplace of James VI.

Fotheringhay Castle, Northamptonshire.
Now a mound of grass, where Mary was executed.

Jedburgh, East Lothian.
Mary Queen of Scots' House. From this house she visited Bothwell and it contains her communion set and other items once belonging to her.

Lennoxlove House, Lothian.
Contains the casket, a ring and the death mask of Mary.

Linlithgow Palace, Linlithgow.
Birthplace of Mary.

Loch Leven Castle, Loch Leven.
Mary was imprisoned here.

Museum of Antiquities, Queen Street, Edinburgh.
This has objects associated with Mary.

National Portrait Gallery, London.
Contains pictures of Mary's contemporaries.

Palace of Holyroodhouse, Edinburgh.
Mary's principal home for six years and the place where Riccio was murdered.

Scottish National Portrait Gallery, Queen Street, Edinburgh.
Contains portraits of Mary, her husbands, family, supporters and opponents.

Stirling Castle, Stirling.
Mary spent much of her early life here.

Westminster Abbey, London.
Contains Mary's tomb.

Traquair House, Borders.
Visited by Mary and Darnley in 1566.

Index

Figures in **bold** refer to illustrations. Glossary entries are shown by the letter g.